ALFRED, LORD TENNYSON

by Michael Thorn

GREENWICH EXCHANGE
LONDON

Other books by Michael Thorn include:

Penfriends, novel
Tennyson, biography

Greenwich Exchange

First published in Great Britain in 1995

Alfred, Lord Tennyson © Michael Thorn, 1995

Printed and bound by Priory Press, Holywood, N. Ireland.

ISBN 1-871551-20-X

CONTENTS

CHRONOLOGY

1809	Alfred Tennyson born Somersby, Lincolnshire
1827	*Poems By Two brothers* published Tennyson arrives at Trinity College, Cambridge
1828	Tennyson wins prize with 'Timbuctoo'
1830	Arthur Hallam visits Somersby *Poems Chiefly Lyrical* published Tennyson & Hallam travel to Spain
1831	Tennyson's father dies
1832	*Poems* published Tours Rhine with Hallam
1833	Hallam dies in Vienna
1834	Tennyson pursues Rosa Baring
1835	Tennyson's grandfather dies
1836	Tennyson's brother Charles marries Sophia Sellwood Alfred falls in love with Sohpia's sister, Emily
1837	Tennyson family moves from Somersby to High Beech
1840	Tennyson family moves to Tunbridge Wells Alfred meets Matthew Allen and calls off engagement with Emily
1840	Tennyson family move to Boxley
1842	*Poems* published Tennyson faces financial ruin
1844	Takes one of many hydropathy cures
1845	Matthew Allen dies Civil List pension granted
1846	Continental holiday with publisher, Moxon
1847	*The Princess* published
1849	Decides to marry
1850	In Memoriam published Emily and Alfred married Tennyson made Poet Laureate
1851	Emily has still-born son

1852	Son, Hallam, born
1853	Move from Twickenham to Farringford, Isle of Wight
1854	Son, Lionel, born
1855	*Maud* published
1857	Sees much of Julia Margaret Cameron during her visit to the island
1858	Paints new summerhouse
1859	*First Idylls Of The King* published
1860	Julia Margaret Cameron becomes close neighbour of the Tennysons
1861	Henry Graham Dakyns employed as tutor for the boys
1862	Alfred visits Queen Victoria at Osborne House
1863	Suffers more than usually from ill health
1864	Garibladi visits Farringford Boys sent to school *Enoch Arden* published
1866	Tennysons look for second home
1867	Hallam dangerously ill, survives
1868	Tennyson changes his publisher
1869	Tennysons take possession of Aldworth, newly-built
1871	Tennyson thinks of going to Ceylon
1873	Made Doge of Freshwater in ceremony by sea organised by Julia Margaret Cameron
1874	Begins working on dramas Emily suffers nervous collapse, ceases journal and secretarial duties
1875	Tennyson negotiates for an hereditary peerage The Camerons leacve the Isle of Wight for good
1878	Lionel Tennyson marries
1879	Julia Margaret Cameron dies Mary Gladstone visits Farringford, has nose stroked
1880	*Ballads and Other Poems* published

1882	Disastrous opening night for The Promise Of May
1883	Edward FitzGerald dies Tennyson made peer after cruise with Gladstone
1884	Hallam Tennyson marries
1885	*Tiresias and Other Poems* published
1886	Lionel Tennyson dies *Locksley Hall Sixty Years After* published
1888	Tennyson seriously ill with rheumatic gout
1889	Writes 'Crossing The Bar' *Demeter and Other Poems* published
1890	Tennyson reads poems into a phonograph
1892	Final illness and death

I DEAD, WHITE AND ENGLISH

Tennyson has been dead for more than a hundred years. By the time he breathed his last, on October 6th, 1892, in the famously moonlit bedroom at Aldworth, he had become a Victorian legend. But there were sufficient clues at his funeral to indicate that the legend itself was in mortal decline. In the days leading up to his death there had been an orderly gathering of reporters, awaiting the latest doctor's bulletin, outside the entrance to the poet's Surrey home. *The Times* correspondent reported that the gate "was made fast by a coil of stout rope." Thirty years earlier, at the height of his fame, it would have taken greater security measures to keep out the curious public. Tennyson's property on the Isle of Wight had been a haunt for souvenir hunters and tourists. When a commemorative tree was planted in the grounds, following the visit of Garibaldi, in 1864, its branches were stripped. It was this sort of attention, as much as the new housing which was springing up at his end of the island, which had led Tennyson to seek a more isolated home, as an alternative to Farringford. Aldworth - the result of a rather clumsy collaboration between the Tennysons and their architect friend, James Knowles - was certainly isolated. Situated high up above the village of Haslemere, it did not have the open accessibility of Farringford. Nevertheless, the absence of the general public at the dying poet's gate was striking. And when the death was announced, no younger aspiring poet is known to have rushed outdoors to spell out Tennyson's name in the ground, as Alfred had done when first informed of the death of Byron.

Despite efforts of the family to publicise the time of the body's transportation by train from Haslemere to London, for the funeral, the platforms en route were empty. And outside Westminster Abbey, members of the ordinary public were hardly more numerous than chapmen hawking cheap editions of 'Crossing The Bar'. High society, including the Prince of Wales, chose to spend the day of the funeral at Newmarket, watching the St Leger, or, as the Pall Mall Gazette acidly commented, putting horseflesh above poetry. Most of those personally

1

dear to Tennyson were already dead. It was an occasion for ex-prime ministers (two were amongst the pallbearers) and elderly dukes and duchesses. The atmosphere in the Abbey was very different over twenty years earlier, when Tennyson had attended the funeral of Charles Dickens, and had been mobbed by a public eager to transfer its allegiance. There was no such impromptu outpouring of feeling on this occasion. Thomas Hardy was in the congregation, but he kept a low profile, and noted afterwards that the affair had been too grand for his taste.

Of course, for a poet, Tennyson had handled things badly. He had lived a long life, instead of dying young; had acquired great wealth and was the owner of not just one but two sizeable country homes, instead of dying in the gutter or the attic; had been, by common consensus, faithful to his wife, Emily, a somewhat prim and provincial personality, instead of consorting with colourful courtesans. And, in the latter days of his fame, he had become associated with many of the least attractive aspects of the Victorian age. Readers of even his juvenile verses find it difficult to dispel the image of the black wide-awake hat, the black cape and the black beard. But Tennyson did not grow a beard until after his marriage in 1850. Many of his best-known poems were not written by a Victorian, let alone by a pre-eminent one, but by a young man from a remote Lincolnshire village reacting to the promptings of a slowly broadening experience. And a significant number of his later poems were written as counterblasts to the age in which he lived.

Emily survived her husband by four years. Although too frail to attend the funeral she was invigorated by a new surge of energy in the last months and actively helped Hallam, the older of their two boys, to prepare the two-volume *Memoir*, published in 1897. Lacunae in the biographical evidence submitted by those volumes have been attributed to Emily's protectiveness and sense of propriety - although Hallam was no less prim than she - and were of assistance to later biographers who were able to dangle their discoveries as if dancing with skeletons in the cupboard. As a result, the Gothic suffering of Tennyson's childhood and adolescence has been much exaggerated and the experiences of his later life have appeared pallid in comparison. Although it would be foolish to approach Tennysonian experience as if it were lived out in the same catastrophic tumult as, say, the affairs of Byron or Shelley, or even Keats; there are certainly poems - notably 'The Lady of Shalott' - which repay a closer analysis of the biographical context of their composition than has been fashionable. His contemporary readers might have affected a lofty disregard for the personal background - the great Lord Tennyson was the English Virgil and the work would stand by itself - but in practice, of course, they were every bit as curious as ourselves, and Tennyson was frequently driven into a rage when writers in the more popular weeklies began to reveal such secrets as the design and appearance of his porch and, in good journalistic tradition, to get the details wrong.

Tennyson's period of fame coincided with the early years of photography. The features and mode of dress which he adopted after his marriage in 1850 were widely caricatured during the last two decades of his life, but after his death a mood of veneration was orchestrated. A Tennyson memorial was erected high on Freshwater Down on August 6th, 1897. A stained-glass window, made by the William Morris company to a design by Sir Edward Burne Jones, was placed in Haslemere church in August 1899. A statue was commissioned from the artist and family friend G. F. Watts and eventually unveiled outside Lincoln cathedral on July 15th, 1905. This was all, in one sense, a very proper response to the poet's death. But writing in 1909, for the centenary of Tennyson's birth, Willingham Rawnsley could already speak of the negative effects which such enshrinement inevitably exacts. "I only hope that the boys and girls and young people of this generation will not take the critics for their guide who already begin to talk of Tennyson as early Victorian and semi-obsolete, but will just read him themselves, and allow their own judgement to guide them."

In many ways this remains good advice. By the time of his second centenary - the centenary of his death - Tennyson continued to be read, if in a somewhat cliquey way, by a loyal coterie of critics and Tennyson

II THE EVENTS

Alfred Tennyson was born on August 6th, 1809 around midnight, in Somersby, a small village in the Lincolnshire Wolds. He had two older and four younger brothers, plus four sisters. His father, George Tennyson, was rector of Somersby and Bag Enderby. His mother, Elizabeth (Fytche), was a niece of the Bishop of Lincoln. George was the eldest son of George Clayton Tennyson who, at the time of his grandson Alfred's birth, was living in genteel retirement on a two thousand acre estate (the product of both created and inherited wealth) at Tealby, also in Lincolnshire. Over a period of time the young George Tennyson had lost his father's confidence and had felt himself to be disinherited in favour of his younger brother Charles. Charles became a Member of Parliament and, in due course, resident of the manor at Tealby, which he had rebuilt in ostentatious style.

Despite their disinheritance, the growing family at Somersby enjoyed more than a reasonable standard of living. George received an annual allowance from his father, continued to draw money from his first parish at Benniworth and, after 1815, acquired a third living at Grimsby. The family income was some £1500 a year and, although the rectory was small, the family employed a cook, a coachman, a valet, a housekeeper, sundry servants and a governess. While Alfred was young the relationship between his father and uncle was friendly enough for them to contemplate joint family holidays at Mablethorpe. When Alfred was four years old his father wrote to Charles enticingly, "Little George can bathe with our children and I have a covered cart on purpose to take them to the sea and for them to dress in."

The older Tennyson boys, after a short spell attending the local village school in Holywell Wood, were sent to Louth Grammar School. Alfred hated it, but enjoyed lodging in the town with his grandmother and aunt. By the time Alfred left Louth in 1820, 'Doctor' (for so the rector was called by his parishioners) Tennyson's sense of rejection had become more pronounced and was threatening to unhinge him. He was in the habit of writing long inebriated letters of indignation to his father

- known in Alfred's household as the 'Old Man'.

The eldest Tennyson boy, Frederick, attended Eton before going to Cambridge. But Alfred and Charles were educated at home, by their increasingly unwell father. It was with Charles (always the brother he felt closest to) that Alfred enjoyed his first creative sparring. They were in the habit of walking on opposite sides of a hedgerow and shouting out memorable lines to one another, and when Alfred was still seventeen they published a joint volume called *Poems By Two Brothers*. It was put out by a printer in Louth. On publication day, April 20th, 1827, the brothers hired a carriage to drive them to Mablethorpe.

Later that year Alfred arrived at Trinity College, Cambridge. The eighteen-year-old who turned up at Rose Crescent, where Frederick and Charles were already resident, cut a striking figure. Friends of his early Cambridge days remembered him as a 'sort of Hyperion' - over six feet tall, with long hair and ample forehead, dark gypsy-type skin, acquiline nose, broad shoulders and moody disposition. He was already addicted to strong tobacco, which he smoked in clay pipes. Tennyson missed the company of his sisters and mother and took to university life slowly. During his first year at Cambridge he began work on a strange long poem, 'The Lover's Tale', based on a story by Boccaccio. It is a poem forged out of intense homesickness accompanied by fondness for an absent sister.

While Alfred was at Cambridge the Tennyson family's problems intensified. Frederick was expelled from his college. Doctor Tennyson turned violent and Alfred's mother temporarily removed herself from the rectory with the younger children, one of whom became mentally unbalanced and eventually had to be shut up in an asylum. Alfred's grandfather and uncle conspired to get the rector out of the country. When he returned, over a year later, he was a sick, forlorn man, addicted to opium and suffering increasingly from epileptic fits. He died, after a period of dementia, in March 1831. Alfred and Charles had been summoned home as soon as the end was near, and after the funeral Alfred slept in his father's bed, consciously aiming to conjure up a ghost. This desire for evidence that the human personality enjoyed a continuous existence, beyond the grave, remained consistent throughout his life.

By the time of his father's death Alfred had established - with his university contemporaries, but not with his grandfather and uncle - his seriousness about becoming a poet. In 1829 he had won the Chancellor's Gold Medal for a poem called 'Timbuctoo'; he had joined the Apostles and formed important friendships with Arthur Hallam, Richard Monckton Milnes (later Lord Houghton), W. H. Brookfield, R. C. Trench, James Spedding, Edward FitzGerald and William Makepeace Thackeray.

Each of these was, in his own way, a gifted and stimulating companion, but none more so than Arthur Hallam, the son of a distinguished historian, and younger than Tennyson by some eighteen months. Hallam, who arrived in Cambridge a year after Tennyson, became Alfred's closest friend, supplanting Charles's position as literary collaborator, and opening up new dimensions in Tennyson's life. Hallam's experience was already cosmopolitan. Tennyson had never been out of the country. He had visited London only once before when, in 1829, he was invited to stay at Hallam's town house in Wimpole Street. The orderly, scholarly atmosphere seemed a world away from the chaos of Somersby. Hallam, reciprocating the visit, and struck by an opposite contrast which presented the Tennysons in a romantic light (he found the atmosphere at the rectory reminiscent of *The Old Manor House* by Charlotte Smith) fell in love with Alfred's favourite sister Emily - an attachment which was to have a significant impact on Tennyson, both personal and poetic.

In 1830 Tennyson and Hallam planned a joint volume of poems. In the end, *Poems, Chiefly Lyrical*, published in June that year, contained only Tennyson's poems. Soon after its appearance the two friends left England for the Pyrenees, part of their purpose being to help the Spanish supporters of General Torrijos, by carrying funds and secret messages. (Torrijos was leader of an expatriate group of rebels plotting moves against the restored Spanish monarchy.) After their mission the two young adventurers took things easy and visited Cauteretz, where

Tennyson imbibed a landscape quite different from Somersby and the Lincolnshire Wolds. Back in Cambridge that Autumn, Tennyson and the Apostles took a more conservative view of the unrest which eventually led to the passing of the Great Reform Bill in 1832, laying themselves open to the charge that, liberal overseas, they were reactionary at home.

Tennyson was, throughout his life, a hypochondriac, and at this time was especially concerned about his eyesight, and went on a milk and bread diet. Later, he joked that he was the second most short-sighted man in the land - the first being the journalist and critic R. H. Hutton. The relationship between Tennyson's hypochondria and his creativity is complicated, but heightened concern about his health often coincided with periods of productivity and, in December 1832, he published a volume, *Poems*, which included some of his most memorable shorter work. Meanwhile, Hallam's affair with Alfred's sister Emily had been complicated by Mr. Hallam's objections, and an embargo had been placed on the two lovers, banning all form of contact. They did, however (much to Mr. Hallam's annoyance) continue to correspond, and on at least one occasion, with Alfred's collusion, sneaked a meeting. In the summer of 1833, at his father's insistence and in his company, Arthur embarked on a European tour. The young Hallam was taken ill in his hotel room while staying in Vienna. News of his death, from a stroke, reached Somersby, where Alfred was gathered with his sisters, a few weeks later. Both families busied themselves with concern about the effect that the news might have upon Emily, who had lost her husband-to-be. After the body had finally been transported home at the end of the year, Alfred did not attend the funeral. Instead, he spent Christmas in a round of visiting and oyster-feasting.

Indeed, Hallam's death strengthened Tennyson's creative resolve. Despite the disapproval of his grandfather and uncle, he managed to avoid any form of paid employment, and was able to concentrate on writing poems. He was helped in this by a fairy godmother, his aunt Russell, who paid him an annual allowance of £100, and by the financial generosity of friends such as Edward FitzGerald. His situation further was eased in 1835, on the death of his grandfather, when he was bequeathed property in Grasby which represented an income of some £500 a year, a comfortable middle-class income.

The next few years were footloose ones. He developed an unrequited passion for a rich girl, Rosa Baring, staying at Harrington Hall, near Somersby. He declared his love for Emily Sellwood, and then broke off their engagement. He descended on his male friends - many of whom were now married and settled in careers - unannounced, and always expecting free hospitality. His appearance, forever striking, now became more shaggily splendid, although he remained for the time being clean-shaven. Still a prodigious smoker, he took to drinking liberal quantities of port. He became an advocate of hydropathy, a specialised form of purgative water-cure invented by the Austrian Vincent Priessnitz, in which the aim was the elimination of bodily poisons through pus in a boil, or through an opening of the bowels, either event being known as a 'crisis'. Tennyson shut himself away in various watering-holes and once proudly announced, in a letter to FitzGerald, that he had experienced a 'crisis' "larger than had been seen for two or three years in Grafenberg - indeed I believe the largest but one that has been seen."

His mother and younger siblings had to leave the rectory, moving south to Epping and then to Tunbridge Wells, which Tennyson loathed. He tried to make his fortune, investing his own and other family money in an enterprise masterminded by Matthew Allen, owner of an asylum. Every penny was lost. The effect of this disaster cannot be over-emphasised. It destroyed Tennyson's confidence; it re-focused his bitterness at being excluded from his uncle's inheritance; it taught him, rather late in life, not to take people at face value; joined to his resentment about being passed over by Rosa Baring, it made Tennyson acutely conscious, and resentful, of the influence of money on the emotional life.

After a ten-year silence he published the two-volume *Poems* in 1842. This contained both new and old poems, some significantly revised. During the rest of the 1840's Tennyson's continual complaints about his health and his relative poverty began to grate on some of his friends. "How are we to expect great poems from a valetudinary?" asked FitzGerald in a letter to a friend. Another of his male friends, Aubrey de Vere, told him that he needed "occupation, a wife, and orthodox principles" and Tennyson, taking the central part of this advice to heart, began to reconsider marriage to Emily Sellwood, having been given some degree of financial security by the award of a Civil List pension of £200 a year (the principal mover in this being Henry Hallam, who had persuaded the likes of Milnes and Gladstone to join him in a petition, following the Allen debacle), and by the increasingly healthy royalties from his poetry. The long poem *The Princess*, published in 1847, although not finding favour with his friends or the critics, sold well and went into several editions, each one procuring a royalty of more than £100.

Alfred and Emily were finally married in the summer of 1850, the year known as Tennyson's *annus mirabilis*, because *In Memoriam* had been published in May, and in the autumn he was chosen to succeed Wordsworth as Poet Laureate. The couple lived for a time in Twickenham, London, but in 1853 they discovered the house on the Isle of Wight which was to be the scene of the happiest years of their family life. Marriage and parenthood - Hallam was born in 1852 and Lionel in 1854 - suited Tennyson well. He delighted in gardening, becoming obsessive about his lawns and constructing himself a summer-house. He was an affectionate father and husband, giving his time generously to the two boys and to Emily who, from early in the marriage, was something of an invalid. She had never been well and her delicate health had been one factor in the interruption to their engagement. She had been further exhausted by two pregnancies relatively late in life. Alfred had to push her around in a bath-chair and manufacture sheltered corners for her in the garden.

Marriage and middle-age both became Tennyson well and, as if to prove that domesticity, had not tamed him, Tennyson's next published volume contained the long poem about mental derangement, *Maud*. After the shocked reception to this collection Tennyson embarked on the *Idylls*, adding to them over a period of several years, working in a small study at the top of the house, then later having a more spacious one built on the first floor. There was plenty of diverting company on the island: W. G. Ward and Sir John Simeon, both Catholics, and the eccentric photographer Julia Cameron, who had moved to Freshwater expressly to live near the Tennysons. There were also regular visitors to the house: Benjamin Jowett, Master of Balliol, Edward Lear (who got on better with Emily than with Alfred), and Edmund Lushington (who had married Tennyson's sister Cecilia) were amongst the most frequent. In addition, there was the odd celebrity, such as the American poet Frederick G. Tuckerman, and of course family visits from Emily's father and sister, and from Alfred's siblings. A succession of tutors came to the island to teach the two boys, the most long-serving being Henry Graham Dakyns, who formed a good relationship with Alfred, and who accompanied the family on one of their summer tours.

Emily recorded all the comings and goings in a journal, in which there is evidence of a sharp change in the quality of their married life after they had, belatedly, sent the boys away to school. Alfred's hypochondria returns. Her own bursts of energy (she had been strong enough to give the boys piggy-back rides when they were small) diminish. She has difficulties with the servants. Alfred takes frequent trips to London. He changes his publisher. He has palpitations and tries to give up tobacco but fails. He drinks a bottle of port every evening. Eczema breaks out on his back and his legs.

After taking possession of Aldworth a sense of emotional marasmus entered the Tennysons' life. In the early 1870's Emily herself suffered a series of nervous collapses, the first of which was set off by a fancy of Tennyson's to take a trip to Ceylon, possibly with a member of the Cameron family, who owned plantations there. Ever since Hallam's death, Tennyson had bored his cronies with declaring his desire to visit distant lands. Like those earlier whims, this one came to nothing and Emily made something of a recovery. But in 1874 she collapsed completely, made the last entry in her journal, handed over her secretarial duties to Hallam, and spent the greater part of her days stretched out on a sofa. Her chief concern may well have been anxiety about his attentions to other women. "Invalidism" was a stock Victorian response to this sort of jealousy.

By this time Tennyson had turned his mind to drama. His historical plays - *Queen Mary, Harold*, and *Becket* - are Just readable but lack the necessary variety of tone for dramatic works. The negotiations with other parties which these productions necessitated, his increasing reliance on Hallam as amanuensis and assistant, not to mention his flirtatious, liberty-taking relationships with young girls, such as the daughters of Thackeray and Gladstone, intensified a gulf that was growing between himself and Emily, whose gloom was made worse in 1886 when Lionel died at sea, having contracted jungle fever in India. Alfred had lost his favourite brother, Charles, a few years earlier, and other acquaintances were rapidly falling by the wayside, giving rise to a sombre sadness which his intimacy with Queen Victoria and his peerage (he took his seat in the Lords as Baron Tennyson of Aldworth and Freshwater on March 11th, 1884) did not dispel.

Sadness and nostalgia are to be found in many of the last poems contained in *Tiresias and Other Poems* (1885), *Locksley Hall Sixty Years After* (1886), *Demeter and Other Poems* (1889) and *The Death of Oenone, Akbar's Dream and Other Poems* (1892). But there is also a vigorously fighting spirit at play in those poems, which pour scorn on his contemporary world. When the vigour finally gave out, and he took to his sick-bed at Aldworth in the autumn of 1892, his dying hours were affectionately if rather morbidly recorded by his daughter-in-law, Audrey. Emily, who had been carried into the room to visit her husband, missed his dying breath. When, a little later, Hallam carried her back in to view the room, it was filled with flowers and Audrey had arranged virginia creeper leaves all about the bed and placed a laurel wreath beside the head on the pillow.

III ASPECTS OF THE LIFE

A number of aspects of Tennyson's life require comment: his family, his relationship with Arthur Hallam, his hypochondria, his marriage, his friendship with Julia Margaret Cameron, his drinking and, finally, his intellect.

When it was discovered, largely as a result of his grandson Charles Tennyson's revealing 1949 biography, that the poet's family history was riddled with violence, drunkenness, madness and opium addiction there was a tendency to exaggerate these themes, so that Robert Bernard Martin's influential book *The Unquiet Heart* (1980), portrayed a man made morbid by black blood and fears of inherited epilepsy. Tennyson's hypochondria was not so single-minded as to dwell for very long on just one possible malady, and there is some evidence to suggest that he did not consider himself even mildly epileptic. The Preissnitz system of hydropathy to which he submitted himself in mid-life refused to treat epileptics, and Martin's case finally rests upon Tennyson's own rather vague descriptions of a shift in consciousness, when repeating a name or phrase. But most people have experienced this.

Equally, the illness and loss of rationality suffered by Tennyson's father needs to be put into perspective. For much of Tennyson's childhood his father was quite sane and relatively well. Not until his adolescence did family life at the rectory begin to suffer. These are impressionable years, but it remains true that there were many light-hearted moments in the household even at this time. In later lifeTennyson's sisters reminisced about what good and entertaining company he could be. He was famous for his impressions, and his favourite party piece was to mimic the rising sun.

Some take the view that Tennyson's relationship with Arthur Hallam was homosexual; that in the hot valley of Cauteretz the two of them consummated their love for each other. This is not open to proof or refutation, but such a view ignores the fact that Hallam was engaged to Alfred's favourite sister Emily - which may be taken as evidence both for and against it.. It is helpful to bring Emily into the picture and to view the relationship with both as a triangular one. The question as to its true nature therefore becomes rather more complicated than simply whether the friendship was 'homosexual' or not. The homosexual thesis certainly helps us to understand Tennyson's reaction to Hallam's death, about which, despite the post-mortem, there was sufficient ambiguity to make Alfred conscious of a sense of blame.

Before arriving at Cambridge, Hallam had been involved in a male friendship (with James Milnes Gaskell) of an intensity which persuaded his father that the association must be discontinued. Henry Hallam saw to it that Gaskell and his son went to different universities. At Cambridge, Hallam was subjected to a campaign by Monckton Milnes (later Lord Houghton) to win him as his special friend. Such special friendships are badly understood by those who have enjoyed the benefits of co-education and the opening up of relationships, both personal and social, between the sexes. At a time when young men were thrown upon their own company, it was hardly surprising that emotional attachments were developed, nearly always of an elevated kind, and that these manifested themselves sometimes overtly and sometimes subliminally. All the evidence, in Tennyson's case, suggests that he only became aware of the depth of his attachment to Hallam *after* Arthur had died. While Hallam was alive, the focal point in their relationship was Hallam's declared love for Emily, and the complicated family negotiations which this obliged. Thus some homosexual component of Tennyson's personality was certainly involved; but whether this ever took a physical form may be doubted.

Quite a number of writers have seen his marriage to the other Emily - Emily Sellwood - as a watershed. All that is worthwhile in his poetry was written beforehand, little of worth afterwards. Apart from the fact that, with rare exceptions, it is usual for long-lived poets to produce their best work in the first half of their careers, this view requires the rejection of too many good poems, including 'Maud', 'Tiresias' and several of Tennyson's very best epistolary and valedictory poems. *The Idylls* are a matter for separate consideration. Others have been unprepared to question the marriage's happiness or to ruffle its aura of respectability. As the biographical outline has indicated, the marriage began blissfully enough, but there was a coolness in the latter years - not abnormal, but not often articulated by those who have written about Tennyson's old age.

Emily was capable of gaiety, but she was never high-spirited. Tennyson liked vivaciousness in females. That is why he had fallen in love with Rosa Baring. And that is why he was amused by Julia Cameron. There are barbed comments in Emily's journal which show that she was jealous of the relationship. Mrs. Cameron was the only person other than Emily in the habit of calling Tennyson by his first name. And he called *her* Julia. He enjoyed her grand gestures and, although he sometimes submitted to them, submitted with a salacious "reluctance", as when she chased him from room to room with a hypodermic needle, it was in the spirit of lovers at play.

A bottle of port a day, as a matter of routine, seems a large amount of drink. Apart from the odd story of Tennyson falling down a hole in his garden at night, or stumbling on a railway embankment and seriously injuring his shin - both of which accidents can be as well explained by his short-sightedness as by inebriation - he seems not to have inherited his father's proclivity to irascible and indignant drunkenness. He held his drink well, using it in the main to oil reflective conversations over a pipe with his male friends. He did in old age become forgetful and sometimes needed introducing to people more than once, but that is a common affliction and one which many old people enjoy playing upon. Several anecdotes about Tennyson's last years suggest he played it for all it was worth.

Although Tennyson belonged to the Apostles at Cambridge, he failed to take his turn at delivering a paper (he was supposed to talk about one of his favourite subjects, 'Ghosts') and was forced to become only an honorary member. Producing a cogent argument and sprinkling it with flashes of wit was not his forte. The surviving opening page of his abortive talk was stagily overwrought. It is possible to see this as a woeful failure of intellect, and Tennyson has been accused by some of a similar intellectual shallowness in his poetry. But intellect plays a different part in the composition of a poem as compared with the delivery of an argument. He used his intellect as a poet should - intuitively. Or, rather, he allowed his intellect to be guided by intuition. This meant that he could be rather naive in outlook. Certainly there was a simple-mindedness about some of his political views in the 1850's and 60's, and a literal-mindedness about the hereafter. He can hardly be said to be an orthodox Christian poet, so resolute was he in seeking assurance about the physicality of the afterlife.

IV   GIRLY WORK & TRIANGULAR RELATIONSHIPS

Tennyson's earliest surviving work consists of schoolboy translations of Horace written inside his copy of the Odes, but by far the most interesting of his juvenilia is a strange, incomplete play, *The Devil And The Lady*, begun when he was only fourteen and revised over the next two years. The play, a Jacobean-style comedy, impressed Tennyson's father - he had keen ambitions for the boys, wanting them to make more of their lives than he had made of his - who found in it evidence of a wide range of reading and knowledge, considering the author's age. The work is sprinkled with schoolboy similes made out of such themes as vulgar fractions and recurring decimals, but is otherwise an accomplished pastiche of adult drama, and early evidence that Tennyson's talent for mimicry was not confined to party-pieces for his sisters' entertainment.

The quality identified as 'Tennysonian' is not a particular poetic style but a combination of preoccupations - memory, friendship, death, suicide, the after-life, exile - already in evidence in his contributions to *Poems By Two Brothers*. That small volume, the publication of which so excited its authors, did not excite the world. It went unnoticed except by friends and Tennyson chose never to reprint any of its contents. The poems can, however, despite their rather 'stiff' - to use Christopher Ricks' description - air of trying-on-clothes, be enjoyed for glimpses of the Tennyson to come. Thus it is impossible to read

> But where art thou, thou comet of an age,
> Thou phoenix of a century? Perchance
> Thou art but of those fables which engage
> And hold the minds of men in giddy trance.

without thinking of Arthur Hallam and *In Memoriam*.

'Timbuctoo', the poem with which Tennyson won the Chancellor's Medal at Cambridge, was really an earlier poem, 'Armageddon', reworked and improved to fit the set theme. It was the first time the examiners had awarded the prize to a poem in blank verse. Tennyson entered the competition under duress, at the insistence of his father. The resulting poem, pretentiously Miltonic, is not easy to enjoy today. Its most fascinating feature is a forged motto from Chapman, used as epigraph, an indication perhaps that Tennyson was conscious that the rest of the poem was not in his true voice.

With *Poems, Chiefly Lyrical*, published in 1830, we come to the first of Tennyson's poems to receive general public scrutiny. They were reviewed in the *Westminster Review, Blackwood's Edinburgh Magazine* and, by Arthur Hallam, in the *Englishman's Magazine*. The collection included a number of what have been called Tennyson's 'girly' poems. 'Lilian' ("Airy, fairy Lilian, Flitting, fairy Lilian"), 'Madeline', 'Adeline', and 'The Ballad of Oriana' are superficial poems, repetitive and almost infantile in idiom. However, they were popular with his friends, and Hallam, in his review, singled them out as a "very beautiful class of poems, on which the author has evidently bestowed much thought and elaboration". This is certainly true of the best and most lasting poem in the volume, 'Mariana', which depicts the emotional state of a young life languishing in expectation of a love that will never come. (The enthusiasm of Tennyson's friends, including Hallam, for these poems may be safely attributed to their eroticism.)

> With blackest moss the flower-plots
> Were thickly crusted, one and all:
> The rusted nails fell from the knots
> That held the pear to the gable-wall.
> The broken sheds looked sad and strange:
> Unlifted was the clinking latch;
> Weeded and worn the ancient thatch
> Upon the moated grange.
> She only said, 'My life is dreary,
> He cometh not,' she said;
> She said, 'I am aweary, aweary,
> I would that I were dead!'

This tight verse structure is maintained throughout the seven stanzas of the poem and increases the sense of claustrophobia built up by the homely imagery (nails, shed, latch and - in the rest of the poem - curtain, blue-fly, doors, hinges, clock). Physical properties are skillfully used to evoke a melancholy mood. Much of Tennyson's early verse about feminine figures concerns passivity and frustration. Critics with a feminist viewpoint have been right to see in 'Mariana' and in the superior 'The Lady of Shalott' pictures of an aroused sexuality waiting to be satisfied, but wrong to interpret them as miniature masques of masculine oppression. It is not just yearning girls who will find life full of disappointed desires.

There were stranger, more philosophical poems in this early collection - 'Supposed Confessions of a Second-Rate Sensitive Mind (not in Unity with Itself)', 'Nothing Will Die', 'All Things Will Die' (like 'The Merman' and 'The Mermaid', early examples of Tennyson's fascination with mirrored dualities) - but none was wholly successful. A short quotation from another such poem - 'Dualisms' - gives an example of a technique still evident in the *Poems* of 1832.

Two children lovelier than Love adown the lea are singing,
As they gambol, lily garlands ever stringing:
Both in blossomwhite silk are frockèd:
Like, unlike, they roam together
Under a summervault of golden weather;
Like, unlike, they sing together
Side by side,
MidMay's darling goldenlockèd,
Summer's tanling diamondeyed.

Tennyson is more often identified with metrical than verbal experimentation and in the revisions of 1842 yoked epithets of the 'diamondeyed' type were expunged.

The 1832 collection contained a larger number of poems that can be included amongst the best that Tennyson wrote. 'The Lady of Shalott' has been loved by both children and adults. So much a Tennyson favourite has this poem become that it has been tempting to read it as if it were by the Bard of Freshwater in the maturity of his days. Widely interpreted as a poem about an abstract conflict between privacy and involvement, it must also be read as a poem about sexual longing and erotic hunger written in 1831 by a twenty-two-year-old who found himself in the midst of an intense triangular relationship involving his favourite sister Emily and his friend Arthur Hallam. Alfred was living in a rooming-house in Cheltenham with his sister when the poem was begun. Hallam had just paid them a clandestine visit. Tennyson's mind was a maelstrom of mixed emotion. His sister was unwell, and possibly dangerously so. Marriage to Hallam and a too sudden departure from the enclosed life at Somersby might undo her. If it were not the death of Emily, it would certainly be the death of his friendship with Hallam. The correspondence of Hallam at this time shows Alfred acting as a brake on the relationship between his sister and his friend, frequently arguing for delay in the marriage-plans on the grounds of Emily's delicate health. In all too real a sense she needed protecting from reality, and from too thrusting and insistent a lover. Although it could be interpreted as perverse to bolt too heavy-handed a biographical interpretation on this poem - a plea for virginal preservation and self-sufficiency - such a reading does clearly place it within the emotional predicament in which Tennyson found himself.

A bow-shot from her bower-eaves,
He rode between the barley-sheaves,
The sun came dazzling through the leaves,
And flamed upon the brazen greaves
Of bold Sir Lancelot.

Rarely can a gladiator have made a bolder entrance. The Lady sees him in all his splendour, though only in her mirror. But his 'coal-black curls' and his 'tirra lirra' song tempt her to the open casement.

She left the web, she left the loom,
She made three paces through the room,
She saw the water-lily bloom,
She saw the helmet and the plume,
She looked down to Camelot.
Out flew the web and floated wide;
The mirror cracked from side to side;
'The curse is come upon me,' cried
The Lady of Shalott.

Part of the mesmeric power of this poem, and its attraction to all ages of reader, stems from a verse structure which creates in each fifth and ninth line a repeat of 'Camelot' and 'Shalott'. The rhyme pattern, demanding four and then three consecutive rhymes, adds to the chant-like effect.

Of all the poems in these two early collections 'The Lady of Shalott' underwent the most radical revision, being given a new ending. In the 1832 version the dead Lady carries a parchment on her breast. The later version has a completely different final stanza, in which Lancelot, and not the Lady, has the final word. Many of the revisions made to these early poems were prompted by a series of crushing critical attacks. One of the most derisory was by J. W. Croker in the *Quarterly Review*. The pity was there were a few poems in the book dreadful enough to deserve Croker's ridicule, notably 'O Darling Room', which it is tempting to hope Tennyson intended as a joke. But there were plenty of very good poems too. 'Oenone' (begun while Tennyson was in the Pyrenees with Hallam), 'Mariana in the South' (Mariana in a hot climate), 'The Palace of Art' (inspired when one of his friends said, "Tennyson, we cannot live in Art"), and 'The Lotos-Eaters'.

The 1832 version of this last poem (as opposed to its 1842 revision) is explicitly about sailors choosing a life of narcotic ease in preference to a hard life on the ocean wave:

This is lovelier and sweeter,
Men of Ithaca, this is meeter,
In the hollow rosy vale to tarry,
Like a dreamy Lotos-eater, a delirious Lotos-eater!
We will eat the Lotos, sweet
As the yellow honeycomb,
In the valley some, and some
On the ancient heights divine;
And no more roam,
On the loud hoar foam,
To the melancholy home
At the limit of the brine...

In one sense the Lady of Shalott and the Lotos-Eaters have

something in common: they live a life of inaction, non- involvement. There the similarity ends. The Lady of Shalott is confined against her will, in a state of innocence, and chooses to escape into the world of experience. The Lotos-Eaters choose to escape *from* experience (they are married, with wives waiting at home) by surrendering to a life of soporific and quite possible quasi-homosexual 'detachment'.

There has long been a taboo against mentioning opium and Tennyson in the same breath. And yet his own brother, Charles, was an addict, and good friends of his were known to use the drug frequently. The poet George Crabbe was a poet who never harmed himself by his hadit. Around the time of writing 'The Lotos- Eaters', Tennyson wrote to W. H. Brookfield, imagining his friend "brooding and dreaming and opiumeating yourself out of this life into the next...". It would seem more than reasonable to suppose that 'The Lotos-Eaters' was informed by first-hand experience.

In 'The Palace Of Art' - another poem heavily revised in 1842 - the poet builds "a lordly pleasure-house" (reminiscent of Kubla Khan's "pleasure-dome") in which to live apart, "while the world runs round and round". The palace is so constructed as to be a microcosm of the world, with all that is foul or unpleasant excluded.

> O God-like isolation which art mine,
> I can but count thee perfect gain,
> What time I watch the darkening droves of swine
> That range on yonder plain.
> In filthy sloughs they roll a prurient skin,
> They gaze and wallow, breed and sleep;
> And oft some brainless devil enters in,
> And drives them to the deep.

I have never been able to enjoy this poem, which has always seemed to me too heavily programmed (Tennyson, in a short prefatory piece, called it "a sort of allegory") and moralistic. Its ending, in which the voice of the soul determines to leave the palace for "a cottage in the vale", perhaps to return one day "when I have purged my guilt", has none of the ambiguity with which the conclusions to 'The Lady Of Shalott' and 'The Lotos- Eaters' reward any number of re-readings.

Another significant early poem, withdrawn from the 1832 Poems at the last minute, is The Lover's Tale. Begun when Tennyson was only nineteen, it had been worked on over the next three years - the period of his friendship with Hallam. The initial creative impulse had gathered various psychological significances and Tennyson seems to have become fully conscious of these by the time he composed Part III. The poem tells the story, in retrospect and through the eyes of the main character, Julian, of his love for a cousin, Camilla. The girl has been brought up in his household as his foster-sister. He falls in love with her, but she becomes romantically attached to Julian's friend, Lionel. Camilla marries and moves away. Julian is tormented by nightmares. Hallam protested at its withdrawal. "You must be point-blank mad," he said. Tennyson was probably right in claiming that it would "spoil the completeness" of his book; but it is likely that his motives for wanting to suppress it were personal as well as aesthetic. In editing the proofs of the book, and reading his own poem closely for the first time, we may suppose that he saw how closely paralleled in real life was the three-way relationship in the poem - the relationship which, in all probability, which had sent Tennyson into a deliciously ambiguous erotic magma of opium-induced sensuality and fantasy.

V DISCLOSURES EN ROUTE TO THE HAPPY ISLES

Tennyson included, amongst the new work of 1842, some examples of a type of poetry which came to be known as his English idylls. 'The Gardener's Daughter' is one of these. However, although it did not appear until 1842 and apparently broke new stylistic ground, the poem was in fact written in the early 1830's, and is another work steeped in the relationship between Alfred, Emily and Arthur Hallam. The friendship between Tennyson and Hallam is echoed in the narrator's for Eustace ('I and he,/Brothers in Art; a friendship so complete/Portioned in halves between us, that we grew/The fable of the city where we dwelt.'); and Hallam's love for Emily is reflected in Eustace's for Juliet. The poem's 273 lines (in its early drafts it was considerably longer) of unrhymed verse evoke the intensity of first love - it was composed while Tennyson was in the throes of his infatuation with Rosa Baring. As a hymn to love-at-first-sight, however, the effect is wistful rather than intense. The subtitle is 'The Pictures', and descriptive detail is applied with painterly detachment. The narrator and Eustace, spying 'Rose' from the shadows of her impressive garden, savour her erotically. It is not until the end of the poem that the reader discovers the painting of Rose about to be unveiled is the work of an old man. This detached, fictional framing of the work sets it apart from 'The Lover's Tale'.

An influential piece in the *Quarterly Review*, written by John Sterling, an Apostle and minor poet, welcomed the new group of poems and compared them favourably with the more austere rural idylls of Wordsworth. "How naked and bare they all are in their solemn stillness!" - Wordsworth. "All that we call affection, imagination, intellect, melts out as one long happy sigh into union with the visibly beautiful, and with every glowing breath of human life." - Tennyson. But it was Sterling's prologue to the review of the poems which spoke most powerfully. In it he cried out for a poet to take hold of the modern age. "The death- struggle of commercial and political rivalry, the brooding doubt and remorse, the gas-jet flame of faith irradiating its own coal- mine darkness - in a word, our over-wrought materialism fevered by its own excess into spiritual dreams - all this might serve the purposes of a bold imagination, no less than the antipoetic Puritans became poetry in the mind of Milton..." Sterling's was not the only voice calling Tennyson to embrace the spirit of his age. Eventually the poet proved responsive to this critical counsel. Other poems bracketed by Sterling with 'The Gardener's Daughter', and already going some way to answering his clarion call, included 'Dora' and 'Walking To The Mail'.

'Locksley Hall' has had admirers and detractors. On balance the detractors have been the most spirited. Recently, Isobel Armstrong has written: "It is hard to believe that the appalling racism of 'Locksley Hall' and the statement that fifty years of Europe are preferable to a cycle of Cathay can be serious positions... Nothing enables one to see how far it is a dramatic poem or whether the virulent bluster has a deconstructive moment. It is partly about the move from hopeful conservative organicism to rancid Toryism but it is not carefully discriminated. If it is a parody it is a bad parody and seems written in deference to pessimistic aristocratic Toryism rather than the new audience which Tennyson's reviewers asked him to reach." Other readers have been able to enjoy what Armstrong calls the poem's "virulent bluster" without pausing to wonder whether it has "a deconstructive moment" or indeed what such a moment is, Biographically, the virulent tone derives both from Tennyson's failure to court the rich girl, Rosa Baring, and his continuing resentment of his uncle's wealth.

The poem, just under two hundred lines in length, is a dramatic monologue written in long, ryhming trochaic couplets. At its heart there is a sense of self-chastisement for the emotional energies wasted on a fruitless affair.

Weakness to be wroth with weakness! woman's pleasure, woman's pain -
Nature made them blinder motions bounded in a shallower brain:

Woman is a lesser man, and all thy passions, matched with mine,
Are as moonlight into sunlight, and as water unto wine -

This can be read as blatant misogyny or ironical self-disgust or most fruitfully as both. The real problem with the poem is that the identity of the first- person voice is given insufficient presence, so that

> I had rather held it better men should perish one by one,
> Than that earth should stand at gaze like Joshua's moon in Ajalon!
>
> Not in vain the distance beacons. Forward, forward let us range,
> Let the great world spin forever down the ringing grooves of change.
>
> Through the shadow of the globe we sweep into the younger day:
> Better fifty years of Europe than a cycle of Cathay.

can be read as "appalling racism" rather than a vivid rebuttal of indolent Lotos-Eating ("We have had enough of action, and of motion we") instincts.

The temptation to give in to indolence found more extreme, and more thoughtful expression in 'The Two Voices', originally called 'Thoughts of a Suicide'. This is another poem written several years before publication, possibly even before the time of Arthur Hallam's death. The dialectic between the cunning logic of despair and the guileless assertion of hope is the ultimate extension of a choice between indolence and action, surrender and resistance. In an early sonnet he had written, "We live but by resistance, and the best/Of Life is but the struggle of the will." The voice of surrender is mocking:

> 'I will go forward, sayest thou,
> I shall not fail to find her now.
> Look up, the fold is on her brow.
>
> 'If straight thy track, or if oblique,
> Thou know'st not. Shadows thou dost strike,
> Embracing cloud, Ixion-like;
>
> 'And owning but a little more
> Than beasts, abidest lame and poor,
> Calling thyself a little lower
> 'Than angels. Cease to wail and brawl!
> Why inch by inch to darkness crawl?
> There is one remedy for all.'

The second, reassuring voice does not enter the poem until near its end, ushered in by a Sabbath dawn, pealing bells, and the picture of a happy family walking to church. The mere mention, by this new voice, speaking in a whisper "silver-clear" of "a hidden hope" proves sufficient to inspire the climactic rapture. Dramatically, this is absurd. The conclusion is, at first reading, too abrupt and its sentimental trappings too obviously engineered, but as so often the case with Tennyson's work this impression is counterbalanced by the straightforward and utterly convincing music of the poetry:

> I wondered at the bounteous hours,
> The slow result of winter showers:
> You scarce could see the grass for flowers.
> I wondered, while I paced along:
> The woods were filled so full with song,
> There seemed no room for sense of wrong;
>
> And all so variously wrought,
> I marvelled how the mind was brought
> To anchor by one gloomy thought;
>
> And wherefore rather I made choice
> To commune with that barren voice,
> Than him that said, 'Rejoice! Rejoice!'

(Leigh Hunt thought this poem the best in the new volume.) But the resistance has not really been so sudden. It is the voice of the poet, frequently interrupting the voice of temptation, which has put up the real resistance.

'The Vision of Sin' was always a personal favourite with Tennyson. He explained that "it describes the soul of a youth who has given himself up to pleasure and Epicureanism. He at length is worn out and wrapt in the mists of satiety. After he grows into a cynical old man afflicted with the "curse of nature", and joining in the Feast of Death. Then we see the landscape which symbolizes God, Law and the future life." But this is a very different vision from the one depicted in 'The Two Voices'. Hope is not whispered "silver-clear" but "pealed"

...in a tongue no man could understand;
And on the glimmering limit far withdrawn
God made Himself an awful rose of dawn.

The voice of the old man, the central part of the 'vision', is delightfully cranky. If he is a cynic, he is a rollicking one.

'Fill the cup, and fill the can:
Mingle madness, mingle scorn!
Dregs of life and lees of man:
Yet we will not die forlorn

Julia Cameron liked to hear Tennyson read this poem aloud: indeed, it is easy to imagine him enjoying the role of the "gray and gap- toothed man as lean as death".

'Will Waterproof's Lyrical Monologue' finds Tennyson in a different mood. Subtitled 'Made at the Cock' (meaning the Cock Tavern, Fleet Street) it appears that Tennyson was not a regular diner there, and the head-waiter, so frequently called upon in the poem, was somewhat aggrieved. Martin, always inclined to find darkness somewhere, comments: "Beneath the lightness of the poem lie layers of desperation." True, some of the lines touch on the frustration stemming from his lack of progress as a poet:

For I had hope, by something rare,
To prove myself a poet:
But, while I plan and plan, my hair
Is gray before I know it.

But Tennyson should be allowed his moments of levity and the general tone is one of boozy bonhomie

We fret, we fume, would shift our skins,
Would quarrel with our lot;
Thy care is, under polished tins,
To serve the hot-and-hot;
To come and go, and come again,
Returning like the pewit,
And watched by silent gentlemen,

That trifle with the cruet.

Live long, ere from the topmost head
The thick-set hazel dies;
Long, ere the hateful crow shall tread
The corners of thine eyes;
Live long, nor feel in head or chest
Our changeful equinoxes,
Till mellow Death, like some late guest,
Shall call thee from the boxes.

A contemporary of Tennyson, W. H. Thompson, said of 'St. Simeon Stylites': "A wonderful disclosure of that mixture of self- loathing self-complacence and self-sacrifice which caused our forefathers to do penance while alive and to be canonized when dead. It is to be feared however that men of this generation will hold it to be somewhat too unwholesome..." The poem is not liked enthusiastically by all lovers of Tennyson. The poetry is fine, not exquisite - it reeks with the stench of rotting flesh. Spoken by Simeon himself, perched on the pillar some twenty years past, the dramatic monologue has some eye-stinging moments, particularly when he speaks of penances suffered before mounting the pillar:

For not alone this pillar-punishment,
Not this alone I bore: but while I lived
In the white convent down the valley there,
For many weeks about my loins I wore
The rope that hauled the buckets from the well,
Twisted as tight as I could knot the noose;
And spake not of it to a single soul,
Until the ulcer, eating through my skin,
Betrayed my secret penance, so that all
My brethren marvelled greatly.

As with the previous poem, Tennyson delighted in reading 'St. Simeon Stylites' aloud, using a voice of grotesque grimness, and breaking out at times in fiendish laughter. We would probably have guessed as much, even if it had not been reported by FitzGerald, so convincing is the effect of the dramatic monologue. Robert Langbaum, a critic who has written specifically about this poetic form, has pointed out that Tennyson's other monologues too frequently invite the reader to treat them as a figure for the poet's own experience. This is the difficulty with 'Locksley Hall' and, to a different degree, with 'Tithonus' and 'Ulysses'. The saint's penances, on the other hand, are so extreme, and so specific, that there is no risk of making a simplistic identification. What relish is at work when we are presented with the irony of a saint *boasting* about his *self- inflicted* miseries! His body is a wreck but his mind remains full of energy.

'Ulysses' was written a few weeks after Arthur Hallam's death. Tennyson confessed that he had transposed a significant part of his own emotional condition upon the imagined classical figure. "There is more about myself in 'Ulysses', which was written under the sense of loss and that all had gone by, but that still life must be fought out to the end. It was more written with the feeling of his loss upon me than many poems in 'In Memoriam'." At the poem's conclusion Tennyson re-dedicates himself to the struggle of the will.

> Though much is taken, much abides; and though
> We are not now that strength which in old days
> Moved earth and heaven; that which we are, we are;
> One equal temper of heroic hearts,
> Made weak by time and fate, but strong in will
> To strive, to seek, to find, and not to yield.

The final line, taken alone, evokes gold lettering on a school shield, but the accumulated mood of the whole poem is far more complex. It has been claimed that the typical Tennysonian character seeks rest through oblivion and, although this poem is full of grandiloquent statement and intention, there is precious little action. And the masculine ambition articulated is ultimately as selfish as St. Simeon's twisted striving. The only satisfaction is self-satisfaction.

> I am a part of all that I have met;
> Yet all experience is an arch wherethrough
> Gleams that untravelled world, whose margin fades
> For ever and for ever when I move.
> How dull it is to pause, to make an end,

To rust unburnished, not to shine in use!
As though to breathe were life.

Tennyson identifies himself with ambition, but it is the reckless ambition of an old man who is ready to gamble all

It may be that the gulfs will wash us down:
It may be that we shall touch the Happy Isles...

it is all the same. This ambiguity did not intrude itself upon the poem's nineteenth century readers, who were inclined to value it as a straightforward expression of moral courage. R. H. Hutton, writing in the *Spectator* in 1869 to counter a recently published article by Alfred Austin describing Tennyson as a 'minor' poet (it was in the late 1860's that a reaction against Tennyson set in) picked out 'Ulysses' to refute this accusation. "'Ulysses' is a figure that will live in literature as long as literature is, and which it argues sheer dullness in the eye of any critic not to have recognized...as marking the highest point Literature has yet reached in severe and stately intellectual delineation."

VI A LIGHT BLUE LANE OF EARLY DAWN

Arthur Hallam died in 1833. *In Memoriam* was published in 1850. Some deconstructive readings of this work have suggested that Tennyson used the death of his friend in a calculated career move. Alan Sinfield has written, "Engagement with matters of faith and responsibility seemed a responsible move for a poet." But he is forced to add, "It was also temperamentally attractive to Tennyson." This view is in contrast to the traditional picture of Tennyson in the years following 1833 - withdrawn, nervously unstable, clinging to his mother's apron-strings and using poetry as a form of therapy. However, the editorial work of Christopher Ricks and others has provided proof both that many of the new poems of 1842 were composed soon after 1833, and that the composition of *In Memoriam* covered a protracted period.

It is interesting that, although some sections were completed in the 1830's, Tennyson did not begin in earnest until after his break with Emily, as if, during the composition, he needed to be emotionally unattached. Even then, he wrote the sections sporadically, - *indeed, Robert Graves, who admired much of it described it as 'a rag bag'* - and between 1842 and 1850 published his long poem about the education of women, *The Princess*.

Publication of 'In Memoriam' was not a step he made with confidence. When it went to the printers he issued instructions for only six trial editions to be prepared and sent to selected friends for their prior approval. Inside each copy was a cryptic handwritten message: "Essentially inconceivably private till its later tho longer brother appear then to die the death by fire! Mind! A.T." The working title was *Fragments of an Elegy*, but was changed at Emily's suggestion. Tennyson did not begin ordering and structuring the sequence until late in its composition. "I did not write them with any view of weaving them into a whole, or for publication, until I found that I had written so many." His re-ordering was essentially chronological, and T. S. Eliot compared the work to "the concentrated diary of a man confessing himself," adding, "It is a a diary of which we have to read every word." (The exact date at which different parts of the poem were composed has provided scholars and academics with many hours of harmless diversion, but at first reading, certainly, and even at subsequent ones, it is advisable to take the poem as it stands.)

The poem's one-hundred-and-thirty-one separate parts, plus Epilogue, group together, according to Tennyson's own structure, as follows:

I-VIII	The poet is grief-stricken at the losss of his friend
IX-XX	The ship carries Hallam's body back
XXI-XXVII	Recollections of walks and talks with Hallam
XXVIII-XLIX	The first Christmas
L-LVIII	Doubt and uncertainty in the face of new evolutionary doctrines
LIX-LXXI	The spirit of Hallam
LXXII-XCVIII	First anniversary of death and second Christmas
XLIX-CIII	Departure from Somersby and third Christmas
CIV-CXXXI	Spring and hope culminate in the marriage of Edmund (Lushington) and Cecilia (Tennyson's sister)

The poem sold out three editions before the end of the year and seemed to answer a public craving for reassurance in a period (exact mid-century) of rapid change and scientific development. Several influential reviewers were somewhat precipitate in acclaiming the poem's religious orthodoxy. Charles Kingsley, ing an unsigned piece in *Fraser's Magazine*, wrote, "It enables us to claim one who has been hitherto regarded as belonging to a merely speculative and pieratic school as the willing and deliberate champion of vital Christianity, and of an orthodoxy the more sincere because it was worked upward through the abyss of doubt." He topped this by announcing it as "the noblest Christian poem which England has produced for two centuries."

There was one sense in which this guise of orthodoxy - yoked - with-reterosexuality had been consciously contrived. The final, and from the point of view of the poem's overall structure, most important period of composition coincided with the renewal of Tennyson's relationship with Emily. The finished work was his letter of seduction - a way of proving to her that he was both sufficiently Christian and ready to join his inner, imaginative world to the outer world of family and domestic life.

The distinctive *abba* iambic tetrameter stanza structure, which Tennyson claimed for a time to have invented himself (and which is now known as the 'In Memoriam stanza'), had first been put to use in political verse of very different quality - for example 'Hail Briton'. The form was not in fact original, having been used by Lord Herbert of Cherbury (1583-1648), and by Ben Jonson in his elegy 'Though beauty be the mark of praise', but was perfectly suited for Tennyson's purpose. The rhyme pattern, in particular, is suggestive of differing emotional states co-existing, and an outward calm concealing a central passion.

O Sorrow, wilt thou live with me
No casual mistress, but a wife,
My bosom-friend and half of life;
As I confess it needs must be;

O Sorrow, wilt thou rule my blood,
But sometimes lovely like a bride,
And put thy harsher moods aside,
If thou wilt have me wise and good.

My centred passion cannot move,
Nor will it lessen from today;
But I'll have leave at times to play
As with the creature of my love;   (from LIX)

If Victorian readers were too taken in by the poem's mood of reassurance, modern critics have been too inclined to analyse from a twentieth century perspective. Isobel Armstrong, writing about the quoted section: "Despite the guarded and subjunctive syntax marriage emerges as a play of power relations which can only be sustained if these are self-consciously *enacted* as 'centred passion' requires relief: 'But I'll have leave at times to play/As with the creature of my love'.

These words bring together both the onanistic nature of sorrow, and the wife's ambiguous status as 'creature', subject, possession, plaything and thus a wife who plays the role of mistress. The ownership confirmed by marriage enables the poet to 'set thee forth', to set up the woman with the status of wife, but also, the strange ambiguities assert, to set up the woman like a kept mistress in perpetuity." This passage, it seems to me, is an example of how effortlessly even a genuine and level-headed attempt to make literature from a different period relevant to a new generation (Armstrong, when she wrote this, was Professor of English at Birkbeck College) builds up an untrustworthy sheen on the original. As so often the case with Tennyson, the real task for new readers is to strip away and rub down in order to identify with the man of the 1830's and 1840's (still a bachelor and still un-bearded) who, for all his poem's subtleties, was able also to write simply and movingly. A good example of the rewards to be gained from reading the poem in sequence is the contrast between sections VII ("Dark house, by which once more I stand"), with its sense of desolation ("A hand that can be clasped no more") and its famous last two lines ("And ghastly through the drizzling rain/On the bald street breaks the blank day"), with its pendant piece, section CXIX:

Doors, where my heart was used to beat
So quickly, not as one that weeps
I come once more; the city sleeps;
I smell the meadow in the street;

I hear a chirp of birds; I see
Betwixt the black fronts long-withdrawn
A light-blue lane of early dawn,
And think of early days and thee,
And bless thee, for thy lips are bland,
And bright the friendship of thine eye;
And in my thoughts with scarce a sigh
I take the pressure of thine hand.

Is there a class of reader not best left to take such sections unglossed?

One more thing, however, remains to be said about the whole

VII THE CHARGE OF MAD MERLIN

If 'In Memoriam' was intended to convince Emily of his sanity and spiritual sensitivity, Tennyson's work during the first few years of his marriage seemed designed to alarm her. Firstly he published, under the pseudonym 'Merlin', a series of splenetic political pieces, some outwardly insulting to the French (there had been fighting in the streets of Paris). His first real activity as Laureate was the production of a funeral piece after the death of the Duke of Wellington. 'Ode on the Death of the Duke of Wellington' is much calmer and more circumspect than his Merlin pieces, but it continues to bluster that the country is no longer properly defended against its continental enemies. It is not a successful poem - its sentiments are too stiffly expressed in a tone that exhibits its effort to be dignified and courtly. Published in broadsheet form to be sold outside St Paul's on the day of the funeral, it found such little favour with the public that Tennyson offered to return his fee to Edward Moxon, the publisher.

Fatherhood briefly induced a calmer and more characteristic vision of England, in 'The Daisy'. "It told of England then to me,/And now it tells of Italy./O Love, we two shall go no longer/To lands of summer across the sea." When he returned to a political subject it was to produce 'The Charge of the Light Brigade', a much more successful and enduringly popular but hardly important poem than the Wellington Ode. Tennyson denied that he had written it to the framework of Michael Drayton's 'Agincourt' - "They now to fight are gone, Armour on armour shone, Drum now to drum did groan, To hear was wonder" - objecting that his poem was "dactyllic" (- x x) but, to be read effectively, so is Drayton's. 'The Charge of the Light Brigade' was written on December 2nd, 1854, immediately after reading a report in *The Times*, and first published seven days later in the *Examiner*.

Tennyson had already started work on *Maud*. Back in the summer he had received a letter from one of his early Lincolnshire sweethearts, Sophy (Rawnsley) Elmhirst, which prompted the reply, "I did not know that Rosa was at Ryde." Although there is no evidence that this was definitely Rosa Baring, the rich coquette who had spurned his attentions, it is tempting to think that Tennyson did see her again, or someone who reminded him of her, shortly before beginning his long and powerful study of a mind turned mad by love. He began the poem in the autumn and continued it through the winter, working "morning and evening". What he succeeded in doing in this poem was to apply his ability to write spirited protest verse, hitherto only on display in occasional, throwaway political pieces, to a work of true stature, and to give full rein to all the grievances that had bedevilled the first half of his life - the disinheritance, the financial ruin wrought on his family by Dr. Allen, and the snobbery of wealth which had rebuffed his advances on Rosa Baring.

It would have been inappropriate to portray a character on the edge, in the midst of a crack-up, by means of a conventional, single-toned dramatic monologue, so Tennyson made use of a shifting, spasmodic pitch, to produce what was termed a 'Monodrama'. The style of the poem was influenced by the work of the Spasmodic poets. Tennyson had earlier admired Philip Bailey's *Festus* (1839) and the first part of Sydney Dobell's uncompleted *Balder* was published in the year of *Maud's* composition.

Tennyson writes as a disaffected twenty-five-year-old, cast adrift by romantic disappointment and sickened by the cut-throat immorality in society. It was an enormously courageous poem to put at the head of his first new collection as Laureate, and Tennyson always stood by it despite the critical onslaught it received. "I've always said that 'Maud' and 'Guinevere' were the finest things I've written." In the case of 'Maud' he amply demonstrated this conviction by reading it aloud whenever a willing (or, in later life, a not-so-willing - the poem took over two hours to recite) company was gathered.

It has some wonderfully demented passages which Tennyson enjoyed working himself up for, but even in its more collected moments the verse is put together with an assurance which helps it to be spoken aloud with ease. These two verses make it plain that we are witnesses, not of an internal monologue, but of a muttered, meandering soliloquy.

The challenge is *not* to read them aloud:

Scorned, to be scorned by one that I scorn,
Is that a matter to make me fret?
That a calamity hard to be borne?
Well, he may live to hate me yet.
Fool that I am to be vext with his pride!
I past him, I was crossing his lands;
He stood on the path a little aside;
His face, as I grant, in spite of spite,
Has a broad-blown comeliness, red and white,
And six feet two, as I think, he stands;
But his essences turned the live air sick,
And barbarous opulence jewel-thick
Sunned itself on his breast and his hands.

Who shall call me ungentle, unfair,
I longed so heartily then and there
To give him the grasp of fellowship;
But while I past he was humming an air,
Stopt, and then with a riding-whip
Leisurely tapping a glossy boot,
And curving a contumelious lip,
Gorgonised me from head to foot
With a stony British stare.

This poem is unquestionably one of Tennyson's finest works, although there is a case for wishing he had ended it at the close of Part II - "I will cry to the steps above my head,/And somebody, surely, some kind heart will come/To bury me, bury me/Deeper, ever so little deeper". Part III (in its original form it was not so divided) adds little to our knowledge of the speaker; and his conversion to the cause of war seems intrusive, raising fresh issues. Certainly the poem invites a reaction in the reader like no other Tennyson poem, and there is little wonder that it befuddled the critics in 1855. From its very first words - "I hate..." - the 'voice' is so different from the tender, gracious tones of 'In Memoriam'.

Despite this, the book sold well. It was published in the summer of 1855 in a first edition of 10,000 copies, and a second was required before the end of the year. But the vituperative reviews and hate mail knocked Tennyson's confidence and reputation back several notches - so much so that he collaborated with Robert James Mann, an astronomer friend who lived at Ventnor, to produce an explanatory essay, *Maud Vindicated*, which appeared under Mann's name, the following year. Emily Tennyson disapproved. A poem "should stand or fall of itself."

VIII   AN EPIC SEDUCTION

Work on *Idylls of the King*, Tennyson's epic treatment of the Arthurian legend, coincided with his growing a beard. Emily applauded the new creative direction, but deplored the facial hair. The first four instalments - 'Enid' (later 'The Marriage of Geraint' [3] and 'Geraint and Enid' [4]), 'Vivien' (later 'Merlin and Vivien' [6], 'Elaine' (later 'Lancelot and Elaine' [7])and 'Guinevere' [11] - were published in 1859. There was then a pause, and the next series was not published for a further ten years. This later volume contained: 'The Coming of Arthur' [1], 'The Holy Grail' [8], 'Pelleas and Etarre' [9], and 'The Passing of Arthur' [12]. 'Gareth and Lynette' [2] and 'The Last Tournament' [10] were added in 1872, and 'Balin and Balan' (1885) [5], intended as background to 'Merlin and Vivien', rounded the whole up to twelve books. (Figures in brackets denote the final sequence.)

Tennyson embarked on serious research in preparation for this work. He travelled to Wales and consulted early sources of the legend. The Victorians loved the poems for their high and mighty idealism and saw the story as representing an allegory of the empire, in which King Arthur stood for the monarchy, and the Knights of the Round Table as imperial missionaries and colonialists. This is surprising, in a way, because, if the allegory stands, the whole sequence has to be read as a sombre prophecy of the Empire's dissolution. Tennyson himself was more concerned with the dramatic representation of individual courage and cowardice, fidelity and seduction, both physical and moral. He called it the war between Sense and Soul. Except in one or two of the books - 'Merlin and Vivien' is almost sensationally graphic - there is a deadness in the language, possibly stemming from the fact that he worked them up from prose drafts, a method of composition he had never used before. In the best sections this uncharacteristic clumsiness can add impact to the set speeches, but it has the effect of stultifying descriptive passages.

As Norman Page observes, the epic's "contemporary fame marked a split between the popular and the critical readerships." The public had

41

bought *Maud*, but had found that work difficult to like. They bought the *Idylls*, and treated them somewhat as *In Memoriam*, trawling their 10,000 lines for moral saws, whereas the critics and other discerning readers were somewhat sniffy. Gerard Manley Hopkins called the whole thing, "Charades from the Middle Ages." And although Swinburne's attack on the poem, contained in *Under The Microscope* (1872), was motivated by a piece critical of the "Fleshly School of Poetry" which he suspected Tennyson of having had a hand in, it is difficult to dispute the central argument - namely, that Tennyson, by removing all reference to Arthur's incestuous relationship with his half-sister, has taken away the tragic magnificence of the story. "Remove in either case the plea which leaves the heroine less sinned against than sinning, but yet not too base for tragic compassion and interest, and there remains merely the presentation of a vulgar adulteress...The Vivien of Mr. Tennyson's idyl seems to me, to speak frankly, about the most base and repulsive person ever set forth in serious literature." The scene to which Swinburne refers finds Vivien, seductress, curled on Merlin's lap and prating the prittle-prattle of the court:

> And Vivien answered frowning wrathfully:
> 'O ay, what say ye to Sir Valence, him
> Whose kinsman left him watcher o'er his wife
> And two fair babes, and went to distant lands;
> Was one year gone, and on returning found
> Not two but three? there lay the reckling, one
> But one hour old! What said the happy sire?
> A seven-months' babe had been a truer gift.
> Those twelve sweet moons confused his fatherhood.'

R. H. Hutton, in the essay already referred to, dealt specifically with Swinburne's criticism. Vivien's purpose was to show the "power which sensual creatures, partly *because* they are without dignity, may attain over the highest and most experienced intellects unprotected by something higher yet." Tennyson was dissatisfied with this defence, because Hutton, like Swinburne, spoke of the Idylls as if the poem was an Epic, which Tennyson strenuously denied. He also denied that it was an allegory, preferring the term "parabolic drift". What will surprise those with preconceptions about Tennyson is to discover that his most ambitious poem, and the one most commonly associated with his image as a boring old buffer, is quintessentially about the power of lust.

In December 1861, just after the death of the Prince Consort, Tennyson wrote a Dedication for the Idylls already produced, a smooth and gushing piece of Laureatese, and in 1873, at Emily's instigation, added an Epilogue addressed 'To the Queen'. Martin comments, "It is hard to believe that the Tennysons were unable to foresee the next move" - the offer of a Royal honour. This was the first move in a protracted tactical game which the Tennysons played to ensure that the peerage, when it was finally granted, was hereditary.

IX SEX, DREAMS & SENTIMENT

A poem which, like 'Maud', attempts to settle old scores, is 'Sea Dreams', written in 1857, first published in *Macmillan's Magazine* in 1860, and subtitled 'An Idyl', a term which, in any study of Tennyson, soon begins to grate, to such a broad range of poems is it attached. *The Princeton Encyclopaedia of Poetry and Poetics* defines the idyl "a short poem or prose composition which deals charmingly with rustic life" and its entry is openly disapproving of Tennyson's liberal use of the term, and the effect that this has had. "Actually," the entry concludes, "after such uses of the term as those cited above it would be rather difficult to say what might not be called an idyl." Idyl or not (there are parallels with Theocritus xxi), 'Sea Dreams' is a startling poem. It contrasts the outlooks on life of an office clerk and his wife, who are on holiday with their three-month-old daughter. In the poem the husband has lost money on misguided investments in a Peruvian mine. He is bitter and inclined to give sensational interpretations to all his dreams. In one dream he sees a giant woman, sitting outside a cave, holding a pickaxe in her hand. Then he sees a fleet of glass ships sailing under a thunderous cloud. In the ships' path there is a long reef of gold. Fearing that the glass hips will splinter and break up on the reef the dreamer waves wildly to warn them off. But on they sail. They touch the reef. There is a clinking sound. And then they vanish.

> Now I see
> My dream was Life; the woman honest Work;
> And my poor venture but a fleet of glass
> Wrecked on a reef of visionary gold.
>
> 'Nay,' said the kindly wife to comfort him,
> 'You raised your arm, you tumbled down and broke
> The glass with little Margaret's medicine in it;
> And, breaking that, you made and broke your dream:
> A trifle makes a dream, a trifle breaks.

The poem ends by contrasting the masculine, agitated, vengeful attitude of the husband, with the feminine, level-headed, forgiving instincts of the mother who closes the poem singing a lullaby to her child. When the three-year-old is peacefully asleep, she asks her husband to follow the child's example. "She sleeps: let us too, let all evil, sleep." It is a poem which only a poet with experience of parenthood and young children could have written, and highlights the insultingly dismissive attitude of those who have claimed that none of Tennyson's experiences after 1850 are of importance to his work.

If any one of Tennyson's works illustrates the difference in taste between his time and our own, it is 'Enoch Arden'. Written in the early 1860's and based on an idea given to him by Thomas Woolner, it was one of his most successful works, selling 17,000 copies on the day of publication alone. A fisherman, long thought lost at sea, returns and, informed by a barmaid that his wife has set up house with another man, looks briefly in at their window and then does the decent thing - goes on his way. Modern readers have agreed with George Meredith, one of the poem's few contemporary detractors, and found the story so much weak tea. As a narrative it spends too long building up for the big moment - Enoch standing at the window of his wife's new home - and then makes too little of it. The sentimental dramatisation which requires Enoch to expire three days after ensuring that Miriam, the barmaid, will spill the beans when he is gone, is risible:

> He woke, he rose, he spread his arms aborad
> Crying with a loud voice, 'A sail! a sail!
> I am saved;' and so fell back and spoke no more.

> So past the strong heroic soul away.

Strong? Heroic? The poem establishes him as neither. A clue to the poem's popularity with its nineteenth century audience can be found in observations made by Bagehot in the course of an essay about pure, ornate and grotesque art. 'Enoch Arden' is used to exemplify the ornate approach - prettifying content which might otherwise be unpalatable. "Many of the characters of real life, if brought distinctly, prominently, and plainly before the mind as they really are, if shown in their inner nature, their actual essence, are doubtless very unpleasant. They would be horrid to meet and horrid to think of. We fear it must be owned that Enoch Arden is this kind of person. A dirty sailor who did *not* go home to his wife is not an agreeable being: a varnish must be put on him to make him shine." We fear it would be horrid for Mr. Bagehot to contemplate the characters of twentieth century art in all their unvarnished plainness. Tennyson did not share this grotesque snobbishness and 'Enoch Arden' is exceptional in the way it colludes with such views.

Tennyson's poem about the death of 'Lucretius' annoyed Matthew Arnold, who believed that Francis Palgrave had passed on an idea he was already working on. But Tennyson had been reading Lucretius aloud to Emily more than a decade before writing the poem, which is based on the legend that the Roman poet was administered a powerful aphrodisiac by his wife

> for the wicked broth
> Confused the chemic labour of the blood,
> And tickling the brute brain within the man's
> Made havock among those tender cells, and checked
> His power to shape: he loathed himself;

The drug destroys Lucretius's ability to gain satisfaction from his previous "settled, sweet, Epicurean life"-style. He becomes disgusted with his petty ways and limited horizons, and discovers his past life never pleased him much anyway. "I often grew/Tired of so much within our little life - /Poor little life that toddles half an hour/Crowned with a flower or two, and there an end -". This powerful poem was, in part, an element of his campaign against the 'Fleshly School'. Valerie Pitt says that it "was intended first to show what a chaste-minded poet could do if he chose to handle 'fleshly' subjects." She then goes on to distinguish it from 'Ulysses'. Unlike that poem, 'Lucretius', she believes, had no relevance to Tennyson's personal life. "It is completely objective; the situation is outside the range of Tennyson's personal concerns." What on earth does this mean? That Tennyson was chaste-minded? That he was frigid? Tennyson has been portrayed in these terms so often - the pre-eminent Victorian, completely in control of animal appetites - that it has become impertinent to suggest that he was capable of lust and sexual desire. But these were such prominent themes in the poems of the 1860's and 70's, and to some degree of the dramas, the creative prompting must surely have derived from preoccupations which had some form of personal relevance to Tennyson.

A reading of 'Enoch Arden' can usefully be followed by turning to 'Rizpah', a poem about a particularly 'horrid', 'dirty' and distraught mother scouring the south downs for the bones of her gibbeted son, a petty criminal. Written in 1878 and in its early form called 'Bones', its eventual biblical (see Samuel 2 xi) title helps to turn the desperate, eccentric woman into a universal emblem of life's tragic doom. Written in frenzied rhyming couplets, there is nothing remotely ornate about the way Tennyson tells this tale:

> Ah - you who have lived so soft, what should you know of the night,
> The blast and the burning shame and the bitter frost and the fright?
> I have done it, while you were asleep - you were only made for the day.
> I have gathered my baby together - and now you may go your way.

The situation is essentially moral, and could easily have been overplayed. But Tennyson is content to assist the universalisation of the title with simple touches (the body is set on a gibbet "so high/That all the ships of the world could stare at him") and, for a male poet, surprisingly vivid references to the maternal bond:

> Flesh of my flesh was gone, but bone of my bone was left -
> I stole them all from the lawyers - and you, will you call it a theft? -
> My baby, the bones that had sucked me, the bones that had laughed and cried -
> Theirs? O no! they are mine - not theirs - they had moved in my side.

'Rizpah' was the poem which finally persuaded Swinburne of Tennyson's greatness. "If after a thousand years all trace of all his poems had vanished from all human record, save only...'Rizpah', proof positive and ample and overflowing would be left...that in the author of this single poem a truly great poet had been born."

Mary Gladstone showed Tennyson a newspaper cutting about a man and wife who had thrown themselves into a river to commit joint suicide. The woman drowned; the man was dragged from the water alive. These bare details were turned by Tennyson into the dark contemplation of a faithless existence which is 'Despair', a poem that shatters any conception of Tennyson as a boringly orthodox Victorian, and resuscitates a talent for biting social comment which had lain idle since 'Maud' and the political verse of the 50's.

Have I crazed myself over their horrible infidel writings? O yes,
For these are the new dark ages, you see, of the popular press,
When the bat comes out of his cave, and the owls are whooping at noon,
And Doubt is the lord of the dunghill and crows to the sun and the moon,
Till the Sun and the Moon of our science are both of them turned into blood,
And Hope will have broken her heart, running after a shadow of good;
For their knowing and know-nothing books are scattered from hand to hand -
We have knelt in your know-all chapel too long looking over the sand.

Clearly Tennyson's own faith and optimism about the afterlife were severely tested in his last years (shaken, in particular, by the death of his son Lionel), and a sense of despair became, temporarily, a recurring theme. 'Vastness' ends in what-is-the- point-of-it-all mood. "What is it all, if we all of us end in being our own corpse-coffins at last,/Swallowed in Vastness, lost in Silence, drowned in the deeps of a meaningless Past?" This was more than just the elegiac mood of an old man reaching the end of his days. It was a feeling which arose out of fierce disapproval for the spirit of progress which had characterised his age, and to which he had given his own voice in poems like 'Ulysses'.

'Forward' rang the voices then, and of the many mine was one.
Let us hush this cry of 'Forward' till ten thousand years have gone.

The monologue was cast as the demented ravings of a fictional persona, but Tennyson, although vigorously denying that the poem was autobiographical in its detail, did own that "some of my thought *may* come out in the poem," and the section which mocked the forward march of literature certainly represented his own views:

Authors - essayist, atheist, novelist, realist, rhymester, play your part,
Paint the mortal shame of nature with the living hues of Art.

Rip your brothers' vices open, strip your own foul passions bare;
Down with Reticence, down with Reverence - forward - naked - let them stare.

Feed the budding rose of boyhood with the drainage of your sewer;
Send the drain into the fountain, lest the stream should issue pure.

Set the maiden fancies wallowing in the troughs of Zolaism, -
Forward, forward, ay and backward, downward too into the abysm.

In the detail of its reference this is reactionary raving, but at the heart of the poem is an elemental, cosmic sense of futility which makes Gladstone's petulant, politician's response (in which he listed all the achievements and advances of the age) somewhat ridiculous. If the tone of the last three poems seems somewhat negative, it is balanced by two late poems of remarkable, oriental optimism and inclusiveness. Tennyson was not afraid to identify himself personally with these. Of 'The Ancient Sage', written and published in 1885, he wrote, "The whole poem is very personal. The passages about 'Faith' and the 'Passion of the Past' were more especially my own personal feelings'" (as distinct from the thoughts of Lao Tse, the ostensible subject). At the heart of the poem there is a passionate disavowal of the funereal blackness which, in our time, has draped Tennyson's image and reputation.

I hate the black negation of the bier,
And wish the dead, as happier than ourselves
And higher, having climbed one step beyond
Our village miseries, might be borne in white
To burial or to burning, hymned from hence
With songs in praise of death, and crowned with flowers!

A young acolyte is carrying a manuscript which becomes the voice, in muted form, for *fin de siècle*, materialist despair. The Sage counters this with sophist remarks about the Eternal Now and references to self-negating "counter-terms", but concludes with thirty-six lines of guidance which reinterpret the forward- striving struggle of the will in terms of spiritual enlightenment:

And lay thine uphill shoulder to the wheel,
And climb the Mount of Blessing, whence, if thou
Look higher, then, - perchance - thou mayest - beyond
A hundred ever-rising mountain lines,
And past the range of Night and Shadow - see
The high-heaven dawn of more than mortal day
Strike on the Mount of Vision!

'Akbar's Dream', one of Tennyson's last poems, not published till the year of his death, is imbued with a spirit of tolerance and hatred of rigid, formalistic creeds.

> there is light in all,
> And light, with more or less of shade, in all
> Man-modes of worship; but our Ulama,
> Who "sitting on green sofas contemplate
> The torment of the damned" already, these
> Are like wild brutes new-caged - the narrower
> The cage, the more the fury.

If these two medium-length poems - together with 'Merlin and the Gleam' and the shorter 'The Silent Voices', 'God and the Universe', 'Faith', and the double-poem 'De Profundis' - are the standards by which we decide whether Tennyson is a religious poet or not, the answer must be that he is, but not the narrow English-Church poet we might have expected. It is, in short, surprising to find the old English male buffer espousing a multicultural point of view.

X   OUT OF THE DEEP

In a brief survey of Tennyson's work it is not possible to cover every aspect of his output. The dramas, which occupied him for a good part of his later years, stand little chance of being revived, and dialect poems like 'The Northern Farmer', whilst popular with some readers, could be lost without any serious damage to his stature as a major poet. But there are several poems of the very highest merit, which stand out from a swift chronological appraisal.

Tennyson was at his most mellifluous in the interpolated songs included in 'The Princess', the best known of these being 'Now sleeps the crimson petal, now the white', its form and imagery based on the ghazels of the fourteenth-century Persian poet, Hafiz. Repetition is a significant feature of this form, so it is hardly appropriate to extract one section of the poem for comment, but the last four lines ("Now" at the beginning, and "me" at the end have been repeated thoroughout the poem) are demonstrative of the obsessive care that Tennyson took to separate and modulate sibilances:

> Now folds the lily all her sweetness up,
> And slips into the bosom of the lake:
> So fold thyself, my dearest, thou, and slip
> Into my bosom and be lost in me.

Tennyson had a marvellous facility for urbane epistolary verse, and there is no better example than the extraordinary 'To E. FitzGerald' (beginning "Old Fitz,..."), written when Tennyson was seventy-four, to the friend he had not seen for years. This is an 'extraordinary' poem, not only because it is so good, but because Tennyson was interrupted in the course of its composition by news of FitzGerald's death. The first fifty-six lines are matey and nostalgic - Tennyson recollects trying out FitzGerald's vegetarian regime, then giving up after "ten long weeks", to feel the return of "That wholesome heat the blood had lost". The outright assurance of "We old friends are still alive" proves touchingly presumptuous. For then "The tolling of his funeral bell/Broke on my Pagan Paradise..."

A similar poem, in that it is written from one old person to another, and accompanied the sending of another poem (the much earlier 'The Progress of Spring') is 'To Mary Boyle'. Here Tennyson is not writing to an old friend (Tennyson had known Mary Boyle, an aunt of his daughter-in-law, for just six years, and not closely, before writing the poem in 1888) and the memories are conjured up by the associations of "more than half a hundred years ago/In rick-fire days" connected with his older poem rather than by shared experience.

And once - I well remember that red night
When thirty ricks,

All flaming, made an English homestead Hell -
These hands of mine
Have helpt to pass a bucket from the well
Along the line,

When this bare dome had not begun to gleam
Through youthful curls,
And you were then a lover's fairy dream,
His girl of girls;

Two of Tennyson's short lyrics have been so frequently anthologised that it takes an effort to come to them freshly and appreciate their full excellence. 'Break, break, break', published in the 1842 volumes, is likely to have been written in 1835, during a visit to the coast. Christopher Ricks has called it a "masterpiece of puzzling plainness". Like other great short lyrics, it expresses more than is stated in its straightforward vocabulary, assisted by the music of its metre *(the extra, fourth stress in the third line of verses three and four is a contributory factor, but this type of poem does not respond to too close a textual analysis)*. The poet does not say that he is lonely. His thoughts are unutterable. But we get the impression that he *feels* lonely, even if he is not *on his own.* "And the stately ships go on To their haven under the hill" - the fleet is in good company, and it is destined for harbour. The poet, in contrast, sees a shouting fisherman's boy, hears a singing sailor lad, but does not want to be like them; he yearns for "the touch of a vanished hand, And the sound of a voice that is still!"

These lines are taken to refer to Arthur Hallam, which, given Tennyson's biography, is a straightforward association. It is what the association leads on to in the penultimate line that makes the poem eternally fascinating, because it is here that it holds back its secret:

> Break, break, break,
> At the foot of thy crags, O Sea!
> *But the tender grace of a day that is dead*
> Will never come back to me.

Every day the tide comes in, but this remembered day will never return. "Tender grace", to our modern ear, are strange words to use about a loved one, male or female. Suggestive of youth, sympathy, beauty (in action) and an almost reverent reciprocation of feeling? We shall never know, but we may suspect, endlessly.

As far back as 1917 A. C. Bradley could decry the fact that 'Crossing the Bar' had been so frequently anthologised and quoted as to become hackneyed. In a sense this was more powerfully true for Bradley, writing as an Edwardian, than it is for us coming to the poem today. It must be remembered that in talking of the reaction against Tennyson after his death we are speaking about his reputation with critics and biographers - he remained immensely popular with readers of poetry, and it was this popularity ("taken to the heart of the great middle class, with its nauseous sentiment, domestic and religious") which Bradley feared spoiled the poem for some readers. The poem was written in October 1889 while crossing the Solent. Tennyson claimed it had taken just twenty minutes to compose. The 'bar' in the poem is, mundanely, a sandbank close to the harbour-mouth, but figuratively the divide between life and death. The phrase "from out the boundless deep", in the second verse, echoes usages in several other poems but, in particular, 'De Profundis' with its "Out of the deep, my child, out of the deep":

> Out of the deep, my child, out of the deep,
> From that great deep, before our world begins,
> Whereon the Spirit of God moves as he will -
> Out of the deep, my child out of the deep,

From that true world within the world we see,
Whereof our world is but the bounding shore -
Out of the deep, Spirit, out of the deep,
With this ninth moon, that sends the hidden sun
Down yon dark sea, thou comest darling boy.

The main objections to 'Crossing the Bar' - and they have been petty-minded - have been to the image of the Pilot in the final verse. In a manuscript note, Tennyson commented, "The pilot has been on board all the while, but in the dark I have not seen him." It was Tennyson's wish that this poem should be placed "at the end of all editions of my poems" and the injunction has largely been followed, although not, significantly, in the first full edition of the poems in 1895, when Hallam reserved this place for 'The Death of Oenone', which his father had described as "his last will and testament".

XI PROSECUTION & DEFENCE

"The nadir of his fame may not quite be reached, but it can hardly be far off," wrote A. C. Bradley, in 1917, twenty-five years after Tennyson's death. Three years later, Sir John Squire, writing in the *London Mercury*, predicted a revival, but in doing so referred to a conflict between "the responsible Bard and born romantic" which was to provide ammunition for two killer-shots. The depths of what T. S. Eliot later described as "a very healthy and natural reaction" were reached in 1923, with the publication of two biographical studies in the Stracheyan mould. *Tennyson: A Modern Portrait* by Hugh l'Anson Fausset, is the more extreme in its criticism, but *Tennyson: Aspects of his Life, Character and Poetry*, by Harold Nicolson, had the greater influence. Both books delivered the same essential death-lunge - accusing Tennyson of being, by instinct, a subjective, lyrical poet who had been driven by the demands of his age into an unnatural objectivity. His "central lyrical throb" (Nicolson's phrase) was clamped down by Victorian rectitude. "The strength that was in him was diverted into ethical, and not, as one might have wished, into emotional channels...The wild unhappy animal that lurked within him had been caged and shackled, and the real intention and meaning of the man had been forever veiled - even from himself...," only to break out in "sudden panting moments when the frightened soul of the man cries out to one like some wild animal caught in the fens at night-time."

Although Tennyson was defended by one or two, the viewpoint peddled by Nicolson and Fausset had a lasting influence and was still at work, for instance, in Robin Mayheard's contribution to the *Pelican Guide to English Literature* (1958), described in *The Victorian Poets: A Guide to Research* (1968) as "an excessively unsympathetic treatment". An earlier defender had been Alfred Noyes who, in *Aspects of Modern Poetry* (1924), told his American audience (the essay was originally delivered as a Lowell lecture), "The plain truth is that a very large part of the recent depreciation of Tennyson comes from those who are unaware of the regions of thought in which he moved." The essay still stands as a compelling endorsment.

Fifty years after Tennyson's death, the tide was beginning to turn. T. S. Eliot prepared a talk for the BBC, published in *The Listener* on February 12, 1942, in which he claimed for Tennyson "the finest ear for verse, in my opinion, of any English poet since Milton." Principally focussing on 'In Memoriam' - "Viewed merely as a technical accomplishment, the poem would be at least an amazing *tour de force*" - Eliot's defence cast Tennyson as "the poet of melancholia, passion and despair" and, in doing so, contributed to a one-dimensional revival. The biographical revelations contained in the grandson, Charles Tennyson's candid biography *Alfred Tennyson* (1949) and the additional background in his later book *The Tennysons, Background to Genius* (1974), written with Hope Dyson, led to the picture of Tennyson as a tortured personality, crippled with inherited diseases, both physical and psychological. Such was the portrait painted by Robert Bernard Martin in *Tennyson, The Unquiet Heart* (1980).

During the intervening years several books of general criticism had appeared. Indeed, the number of 'Tennyson' titles published after 1940 was the surest indication of his revival. *Tennyson in America* (1943) by John O. Eidson demonstrated that the poet's high reputation there (Edgar Allen Poe had considered him the greatest poet ever produced by England) had developed independently and in advance of his home reputation. Jerome H. Buckley's *Tennyson: The Growth of a Poet* (1960) was the first to take full benefit of the papers held in the Houghton Library (these include 650 drafts of 350 poems contained in 72 notebooks and nearly 300 folders of loose manuscripts), and in England close textual study of the poems was undertaken by Christopher Ricks, who edited the first scholarly edition of the complete poems in 1969 (a three-volume second edition appearing in 1987) and published a short general study *Tennyson* (1972). It was in this book that Ricks, in ending his biographical survey of Tennyson's life in the year 1850, gave renewed credence to the notion that "By the 1850s Tennyson... had undergone all that truly formed him." A volume which did concentrate on the biographical details of Tennyson's later life, by making extensive use of Emily Tennyson's diary and correspondence, was Joanna Richardson's *Pre-eminent Victorian: A Study in Tennyson* (1962). This was a book which further placed Tennyson as prime symbol of the Victorian age. Published in the same year and giving equal weighting to the whole life was *Tennyson Laureate* by Valerie Pitt - this contains valuable critical studies of most of the poems, but is not factually reliable.

Alan Sinfield's *Alfred Tennyson* (1986) is an application of "materialist deconstruction" to a reading of Tennyson's work, which turns itself into a political pamphlet arguing for the study of literature to be "reconstituted as a technique of suspicion", so that there is an "opportunity for the intellectual to develop techniques for seeing through what those in power are telling us, have been telling us for centuries." Isobel Armstrong's essays on Tennyson in her book *Victorian Poetry* (1993) are infected with the same agenda. The scrupulous notes to these two books bear witness to the the detailed scholarly attention which Tennyson has received over the past fifty years.

The most recent biographies are *Tennyson* (1992) by Michael Thorn and *Tennyson* (1993) by Peter Levi, both rich in anecdotal detail, little of which tallies with the view of Tennyson as morbidly enfeebled. That his poetry is suffused with a sense of shame is made much of by Eric Griffiths in *The Printed Voice of Victorian Poetry* (1989), in which he shows that Tennyson's morbidity was not a sickness or disease, but a "fixity of temperament" bound up with his desire for survival. Tennyson's survival in the public domain, however, *is* tenaciously morbid, in the sense of his work being most frequently quoted in the context of requiem. In an episode of *Neighbours* a character in mourning was sent a bouquet of flowers - the quotation on the card was from 'In Memoriam'. In the film *JFK*, Jim Garrison (acted by Kevin Costner) is made to quote from 'Idylls of the King' in his peroration to the jury - indeed, the Camelot iconology which enveloped the Kennedy family (particularly in retrospect, after the assassinations of John and Robert) was essentially Tennysonian.

Despite the rebuilding of Tennyson's literary reputation, those general readers who know the full range of his work are probably still too few in number to shift this image in favour of other registers. If, when reading the Romantic poets, the challenge is to try and make sense of a range of heightened, stylised images from various sensational interpretations of their lives, and to hold them still, the challenge when reading Tennyson is quite different - it is to take one of the black-and-white images of the becloaked and bearded laureate, to blow away the accumulated, constraining dust of sober, Victorian stereotypes and make Tennyson move again as a young, clean-shaven undergraduate; a footloose bachelor, cheated in love and money, haunted by the memory of Arthur Hallam, playing will-I won't-I marry Emily; then the doting husband and parent; the controversial laureate; the demonic caricatured chanter of *Maud*; the subject of Julia Margaret Cameron's attentive but not so innocent playfulness; the earnest writer of idylls and dramas; the socially inept port-drinker; the stroker of young girls' noses; the slowly estranged partner of an invalid wife; amateur star-gazer; speculative thinker desperately seeking reassurance that there is something, a gleam still to follow, beyond death... and, by so making Tennyson move again, be moved by him, and by his work.

Not of the sunlight,
Not of the moonlight,
Not of the starlight!
O young Mariner,
Down to the haven,
Call your companions,
Launch your vessel,
And crowd your canvas,
And, ere it vanishes
Over the margin,
After it, follow it,
Follow The Gleam.

SELECT BIBLIOGRAPHY

Hallam Tennyson *Alfred Lord Tennyson: A Memoir* (1897)

Charles Tennyson *Alfred Tennyson* (1949)

Jerome Buckley Tennyson: *The Growth Of A Poet* (1960)

ed. John Jump Tennyson, *The Critical Heritage* (1967)

Christopher Ricks *Tennyson* (1972)

Charles Tennyson and Hope Dyson *The Tennysons: Background To Genius* (1974)

June Steffensen Hagen *Tennyson & His Publishers* (1979)

Robert Bernard Martin *The Unquiet Heart* (1980)

ed. Lang & Shannon *The Letters Of Alfred Lord Tennyson, 3 vol5* (1982, 1987, 1990)

Norman Page *Tennyson: Interviews & Recollections* (1983)

Alan Sinfield *Alfred Tennyson* (1986)

Michael Thorn *Tennyson* (1992)